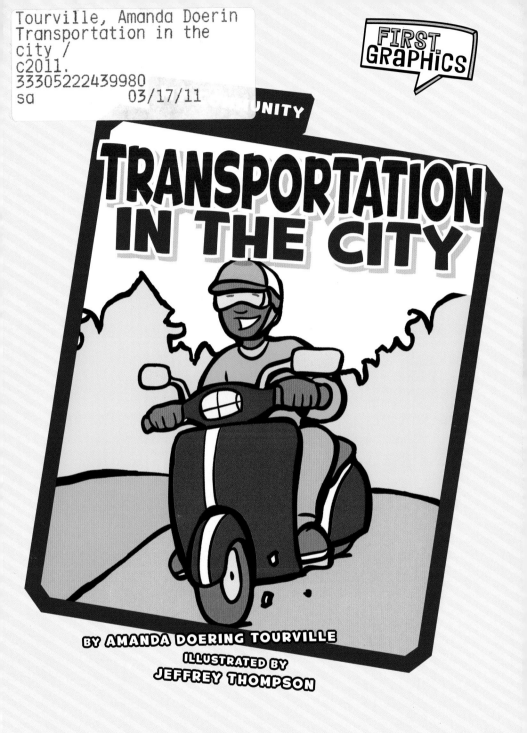

TRANSPORTATION IN THE CITY

BY AMANDA DOERING TOURVILLE

ILLUSTRATED BY
JEFFREY THOMPSON

CAPSTONE PRESS
a capstone imprint

First Graphics are published by Capstone Press,
151 Good Counsel Drive, P.O. Box 669, Mankato, Minnesota 56002.
www.capstonepub.com

Books published by Capstone Press are manufactured with paper containing at least 10 percent post-consumer waste.

Library of Congress Cataloging-in-Publication Data
Tourville, Amanda Doering, 1980–
Transportation in the city / by Amanda Doering Tourville ; illustrated by Jeffrey Thompson.
p. cm. — (First graphics. My community)
Summary: "In graphic novel format, text and illustrations describe a trip on many different kinds of transportation in the city"—Provided by publisher.
ISBN 978-1-4296-5370-1 (library binding)
ISBN 978-1-4296-6233-8 (paperback)
1. Urban transportation—Comic books, strips, etc.—Juvenile literature. I. Thompson, Jeffrey (Jeffrey Allen), 1970– II. Title. III. Series.

HE305.T679 2011 2010026749
388.4—dc22

Editor: **Shelly Lyons**
Designer: **Alison Thiele**
Art Director: **Nathan Gassman**
Production Specialist: **Eric Manske**

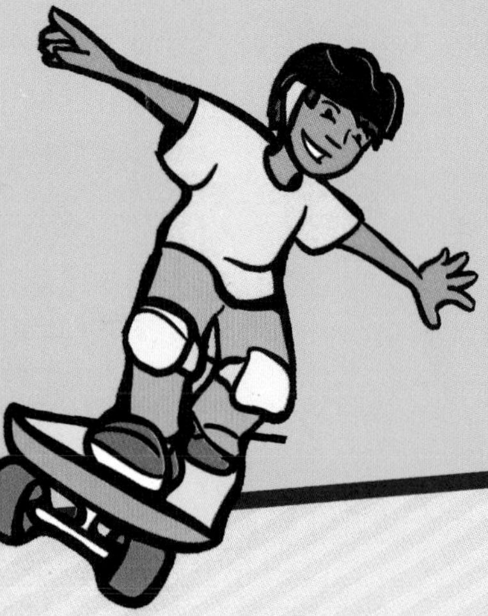

Printed in the United States of America in
Stevens Point, Wisconsin.
092010 005934WZS11

TABLE OF CONTENTS

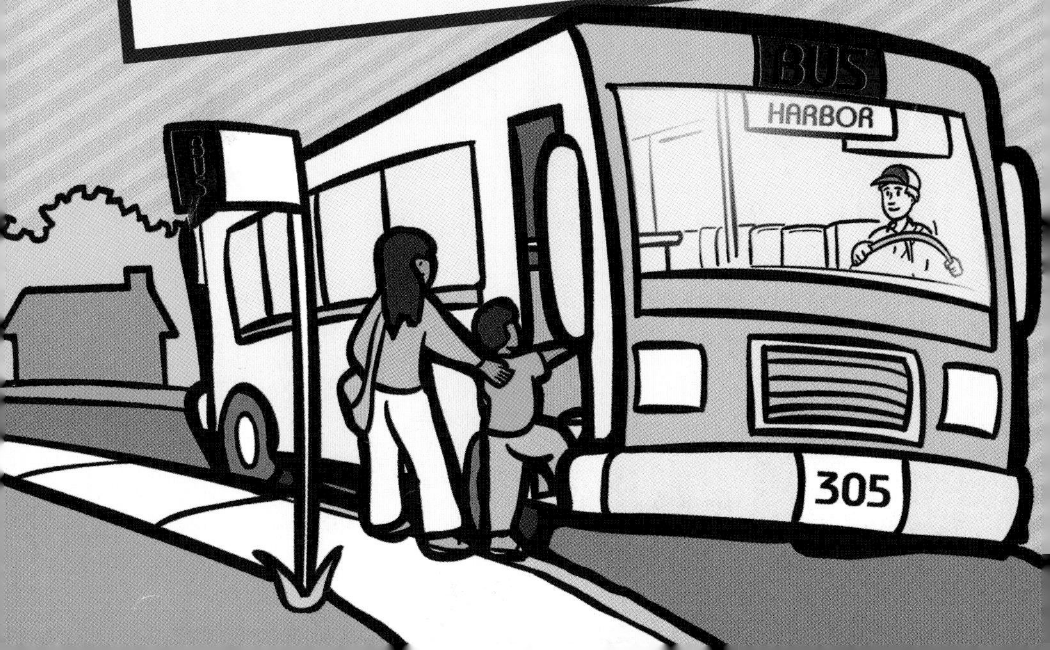

BUS
HARBOR
305

Getting Around

Many kinds of transportation carry people from one place to another. In big cities, there are several ways to get around.

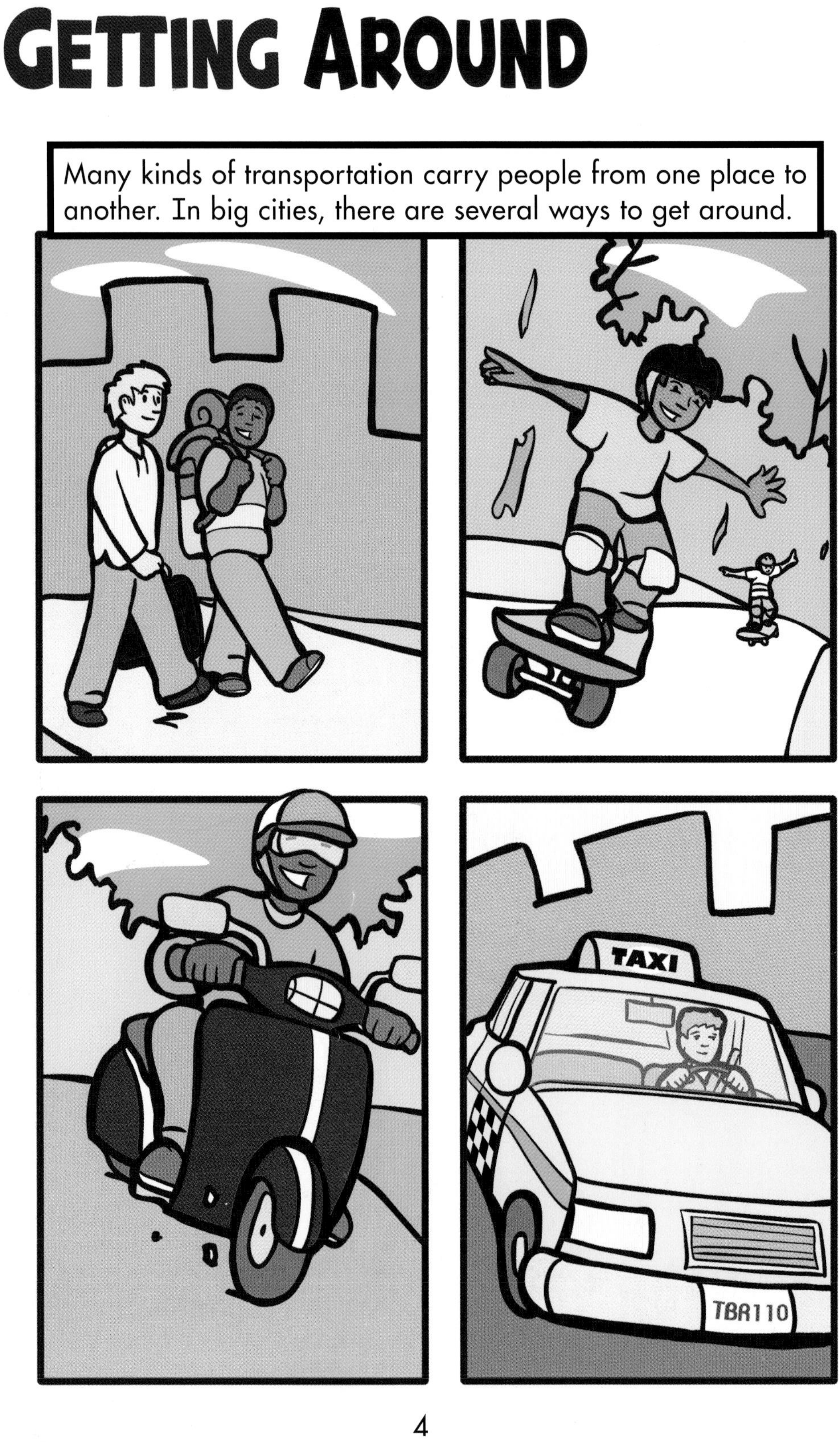
TAXI
TBR110

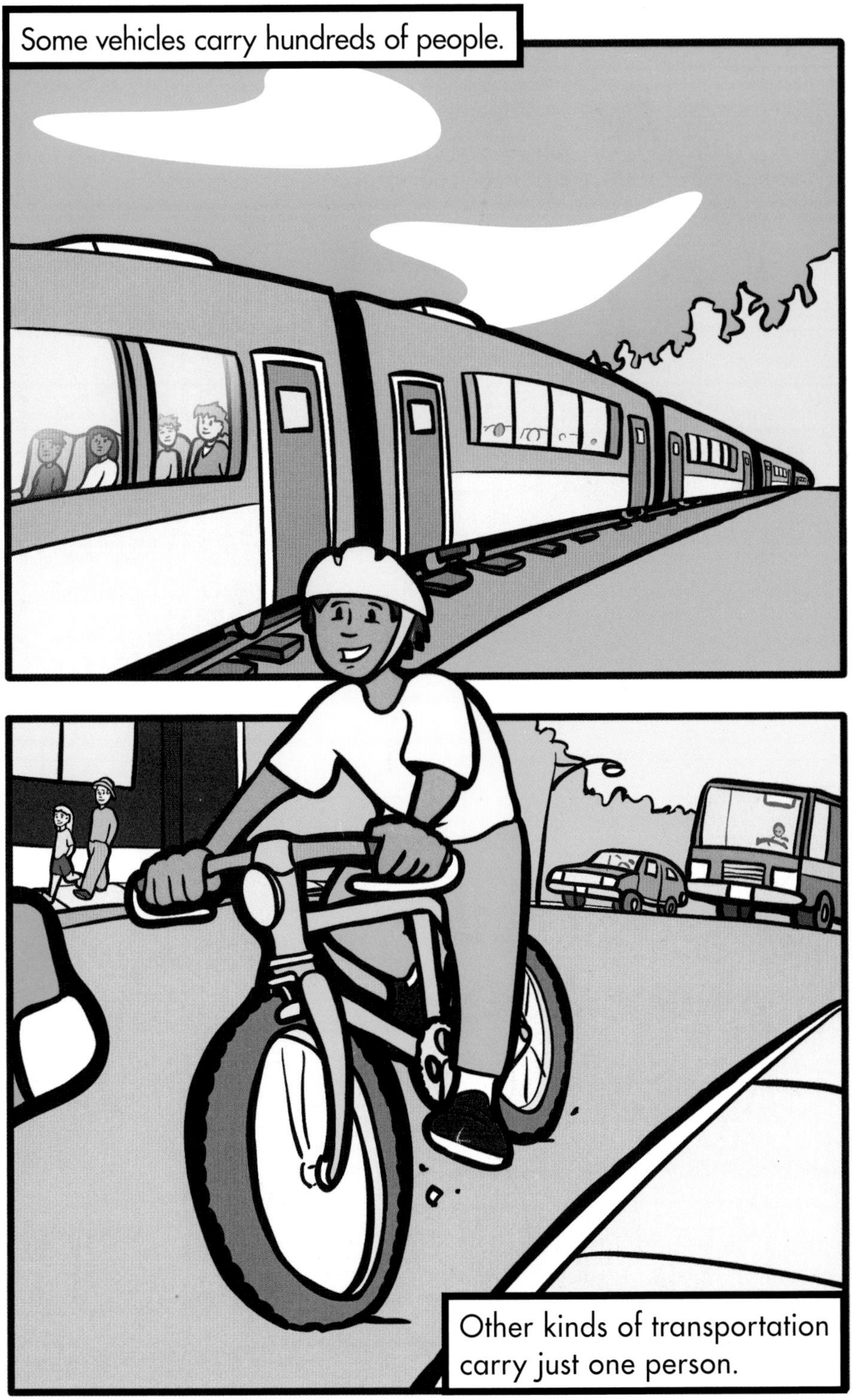
Some vehicles carry hundreds of people.
Other kinds of transportation carry just one person.

Moving Many People

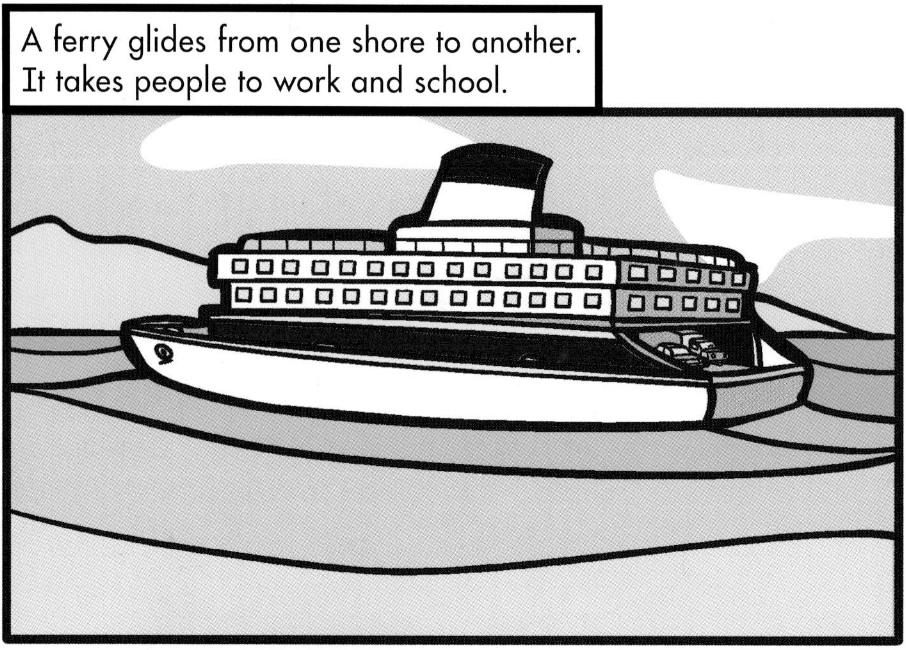
A ferry glides from one shore to another. It takes people to work and school.

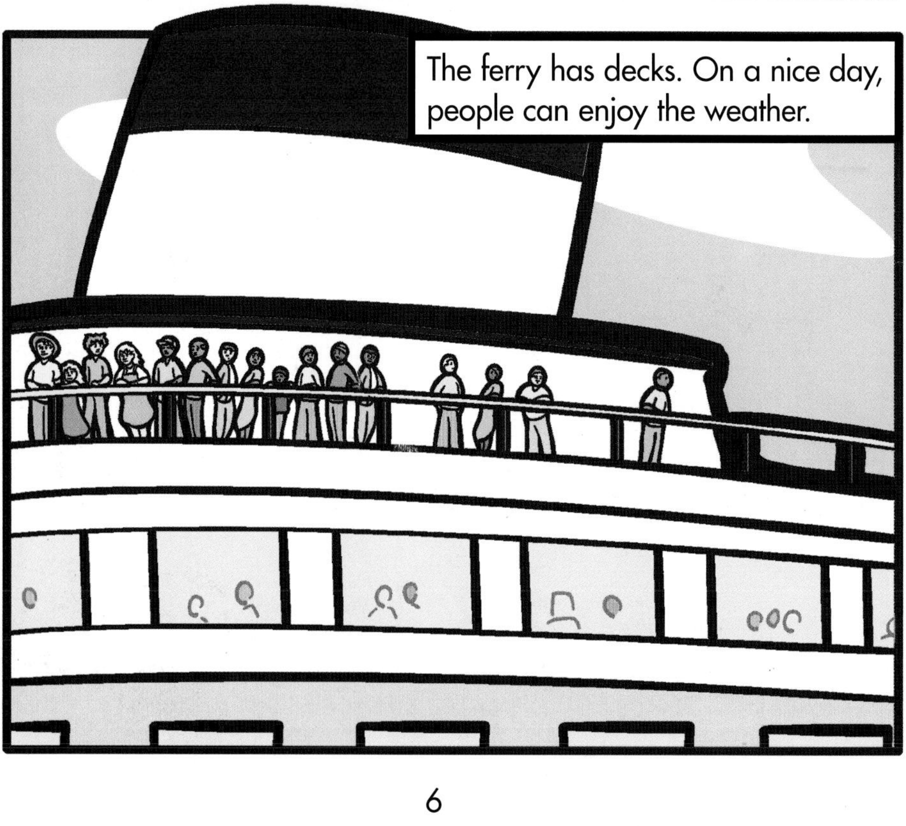
The ferry has decks. On a nice day, people can enjoy the weather.

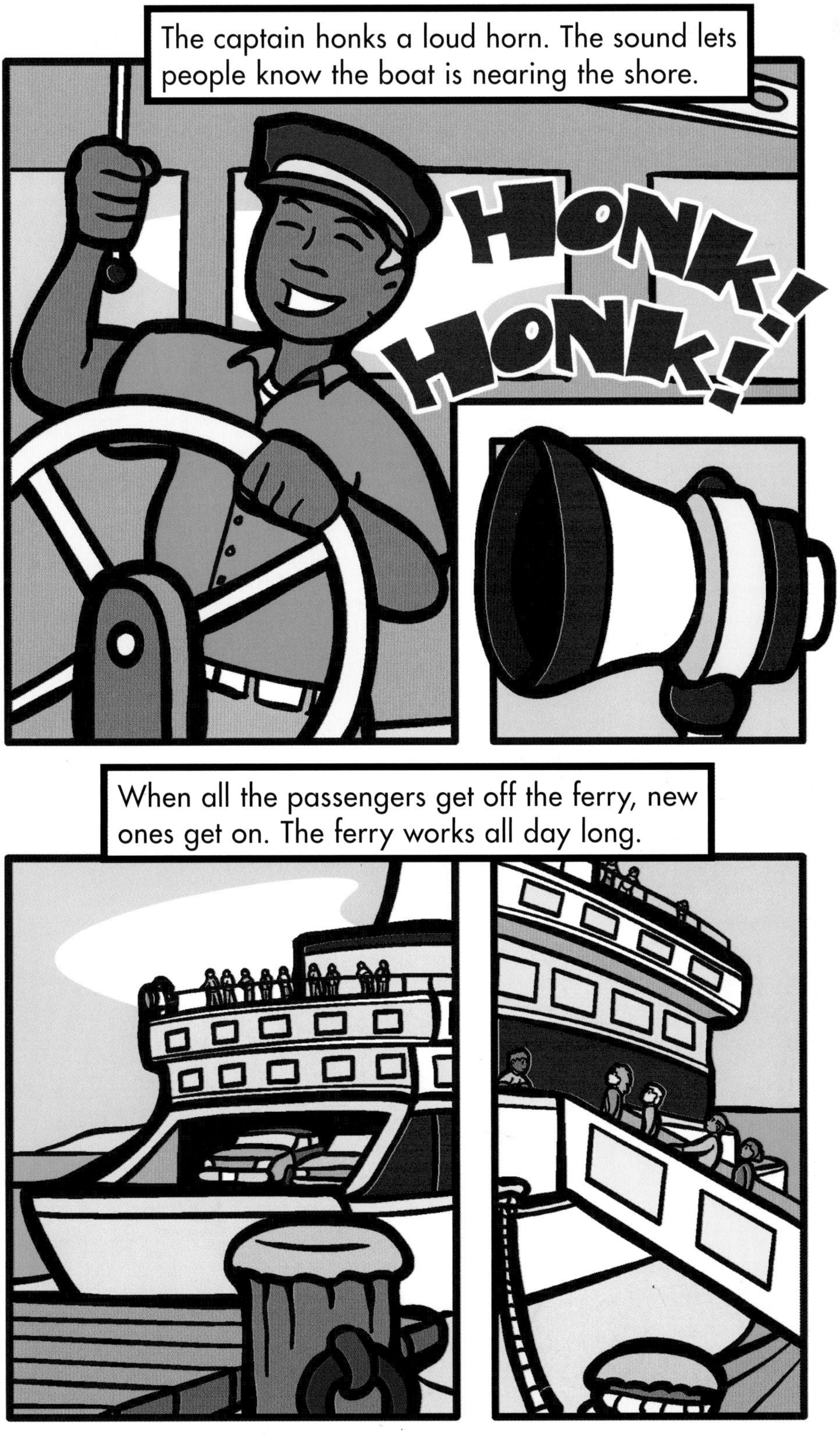
The captain honks a loud horn. The sound lets people know the boat is nearing the shore.
HONK! HONK!
When all the passengers get off the ferry, new ones get on. The ferry works all day long.

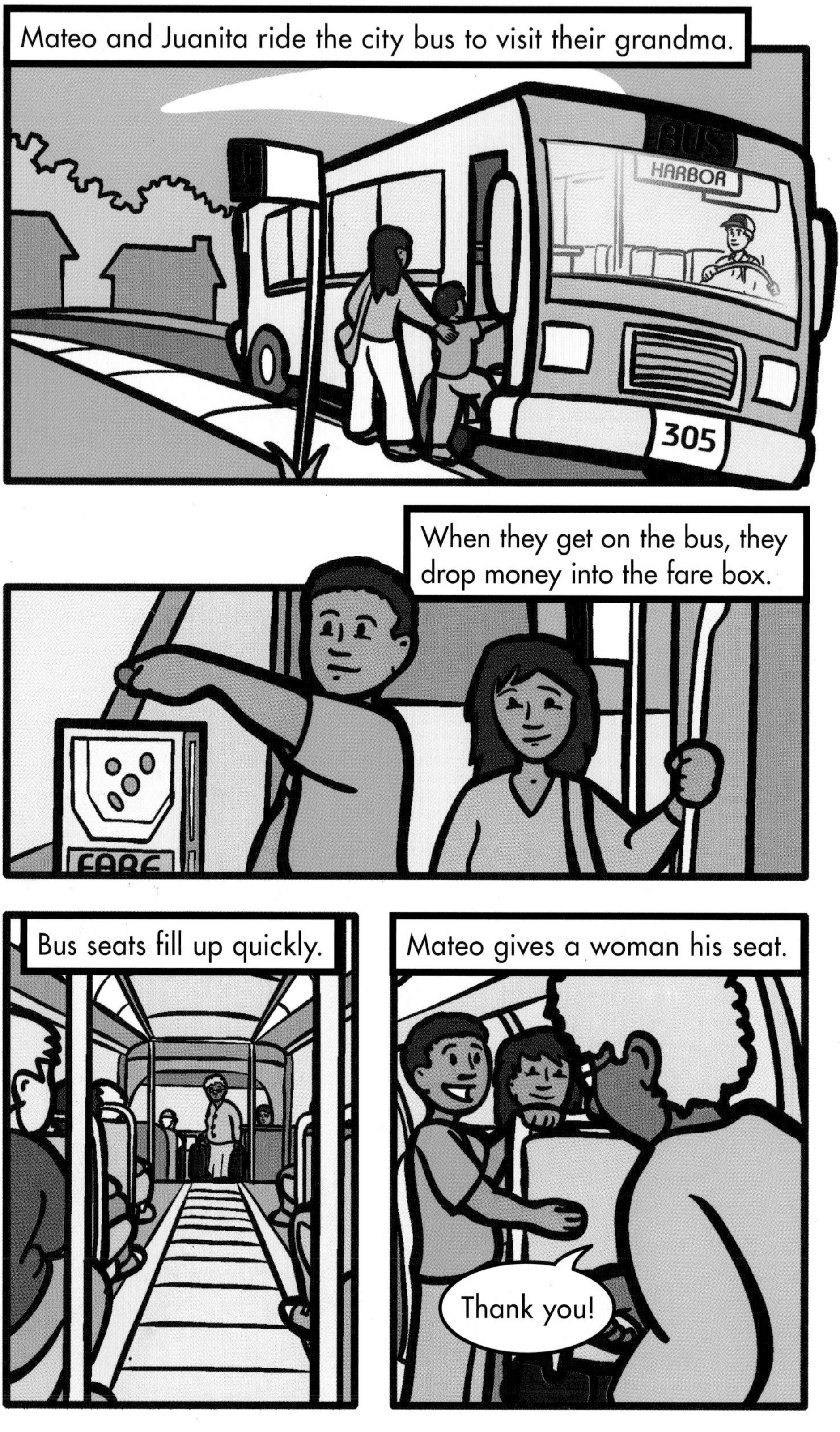
Mateo and Juanita ride the city bus to visit their grandma.
BUS
HARBOR
305
When they get on the bus, they drop money into the fare box.
Bus seats fill up quickly.
Mateo gives a woman his seat.
Thank you!

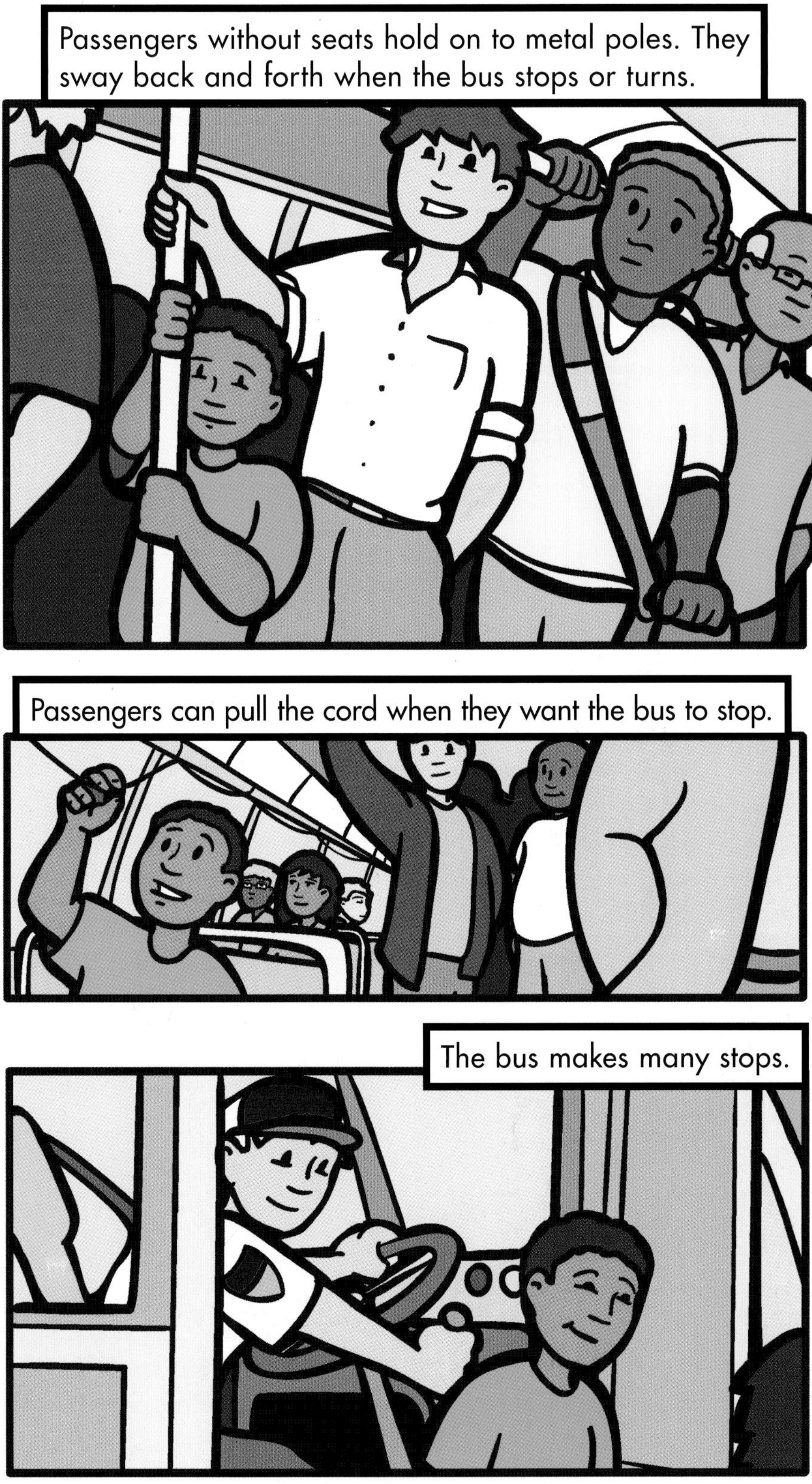
Passengers without seats hold on to metal poles. They sway back and forth when the bus stops or turns.
Passengers can pull the cord when they want the bus to stop.
The bus makes many stops.

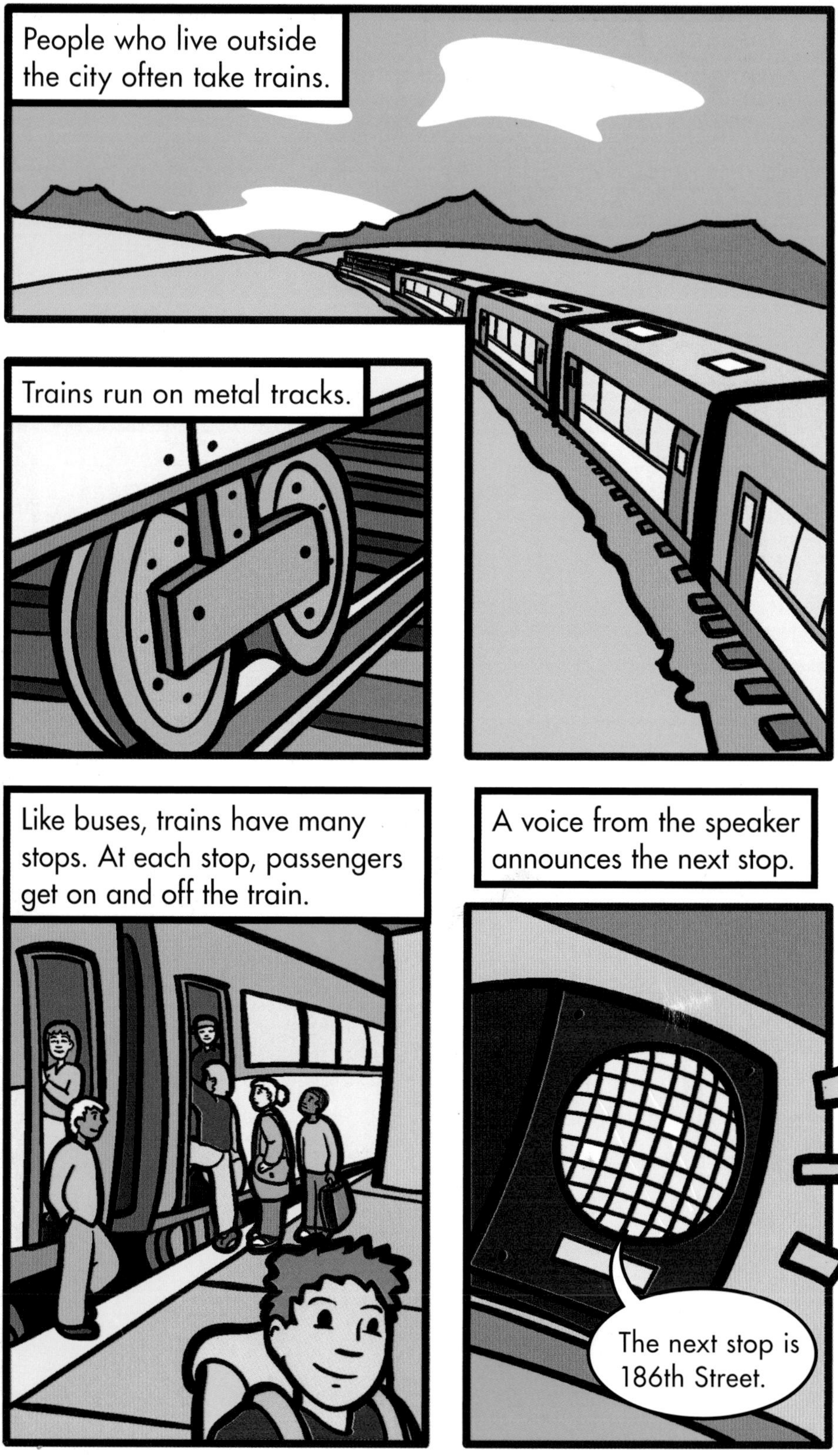
People who live outside the city often take trains.
Trains run on metal tracks.
Like buses, trains have many stops. At each stop, passengers get on and off the train.
A voice from the speaker announces the next stop.
The next stop is 186th Street.

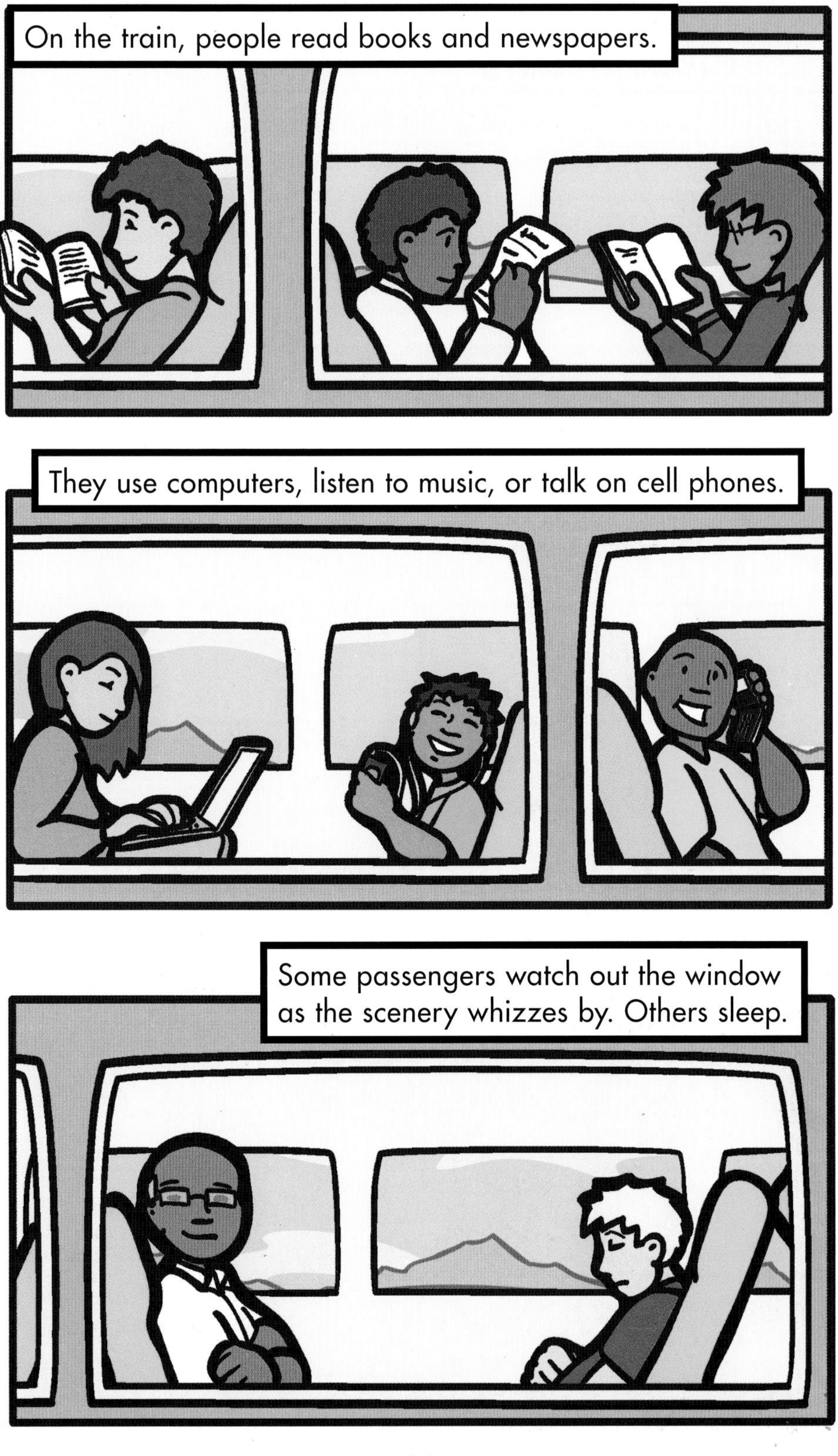
On the train, people read books and newspapers.
They use computers, listen to music, or talk on cell phones.
Some passengers watch out the window as the scenery whizzes by. Others sleep.

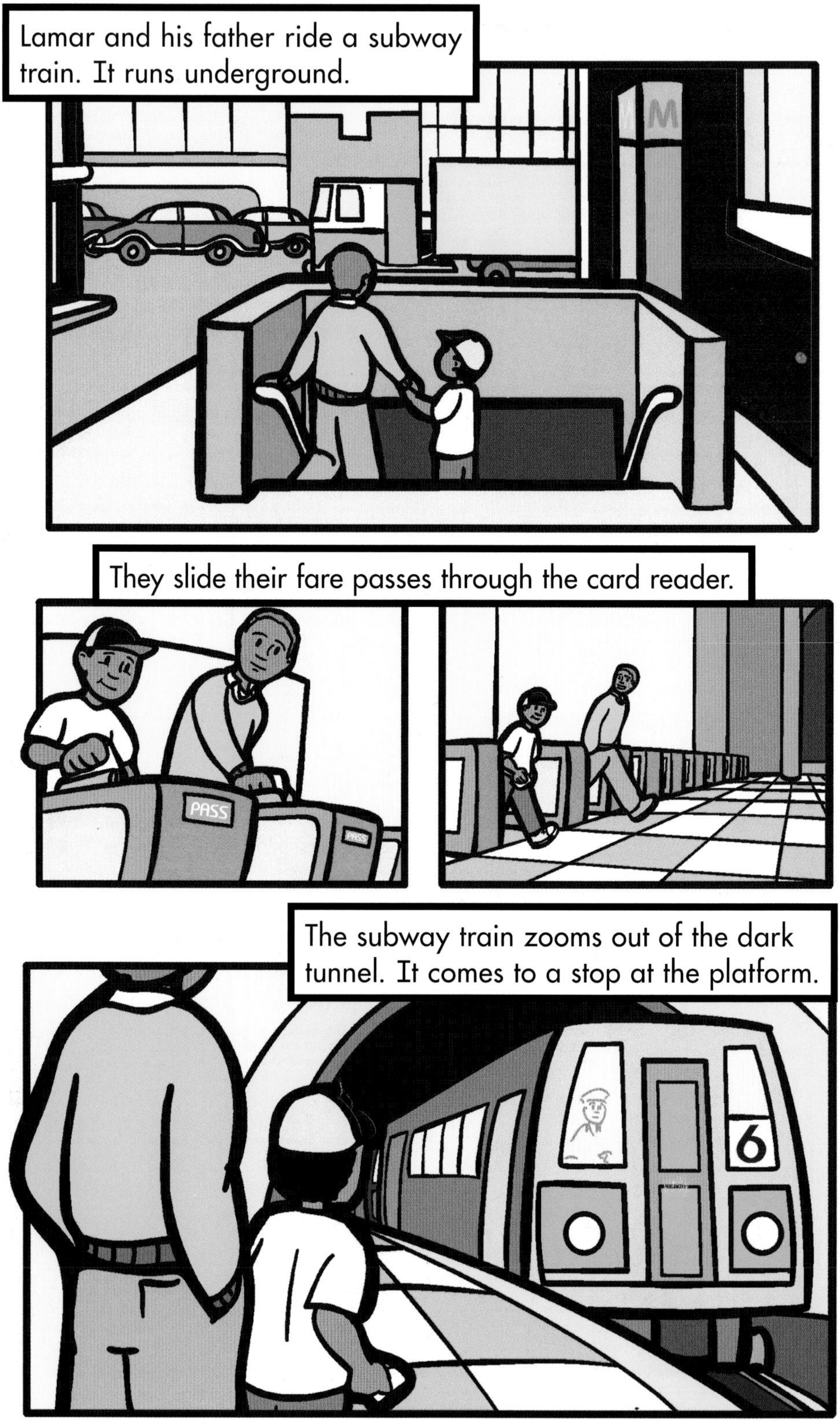
Lamar and his father ride a subway train. It runs underground.
M
They slide their fare passes through the card reader.
PASS
PASS
The subway train zooms out of the dark tunnel. It comes to a stop at the platform.
6

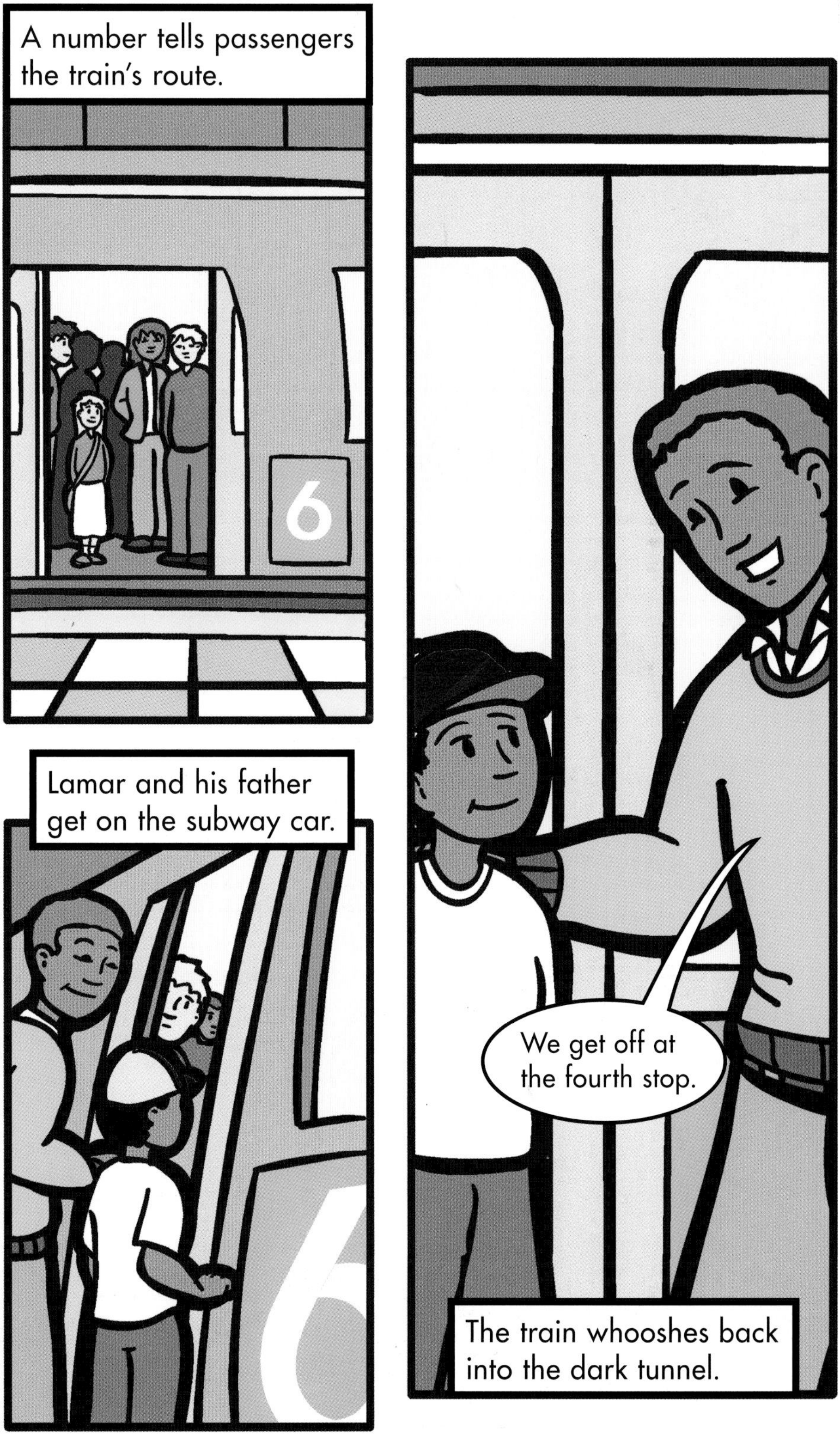
A number tells passengers the train's route.
6
Lamar and his father get on the subway car.
6
We get off at the fourth stop.
The train whooshes back into the dark tunnel.

By Car

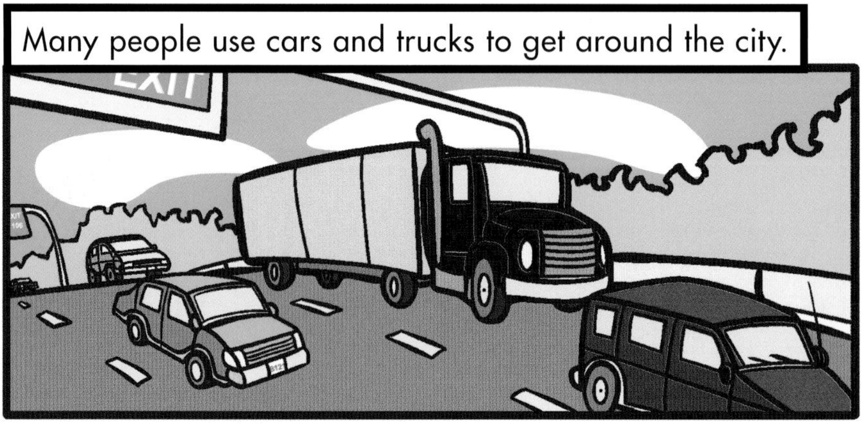
Many people use cars and trucks to get around the city.

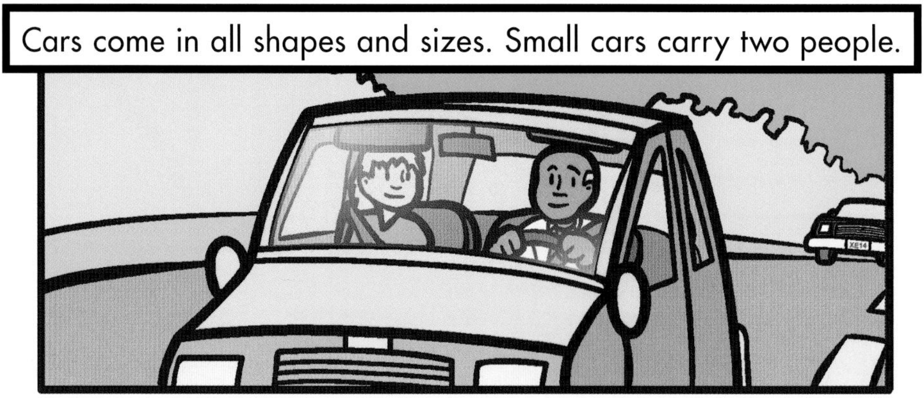
Cars come in all shapes and sizes. Small cars carry two people.

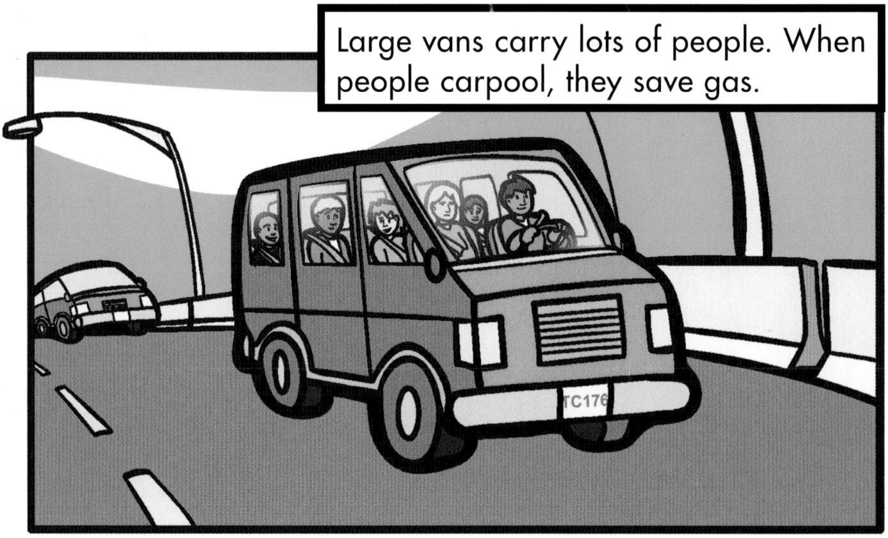
Large vans carry lots of people. When people carpool, they save gas.
TC176

When vehicles crowd a road, traffic jams can happen. In a traffic jam, cars and trucks move very slowly, or not at all.

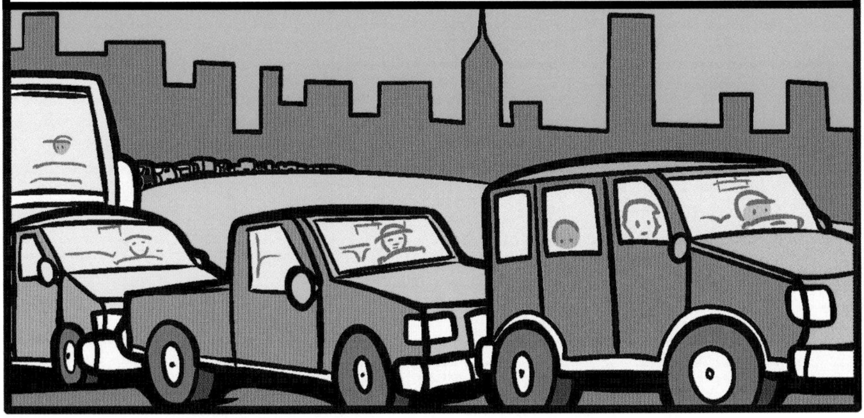

Some people use taxis to get around. Taxis are often brightly colored cars or vans.

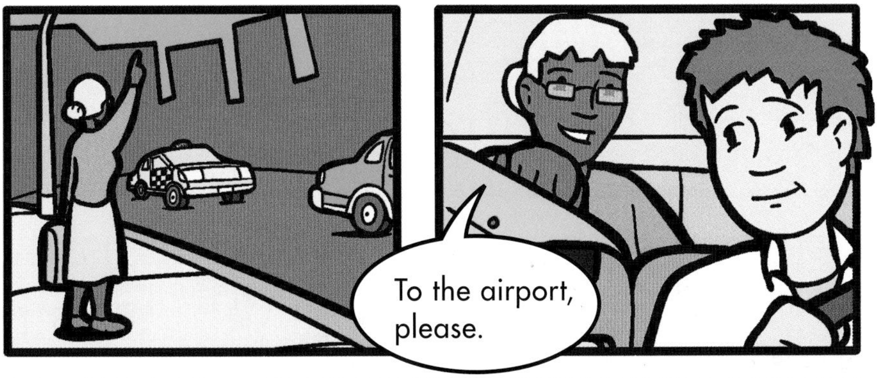
To the airport, please.

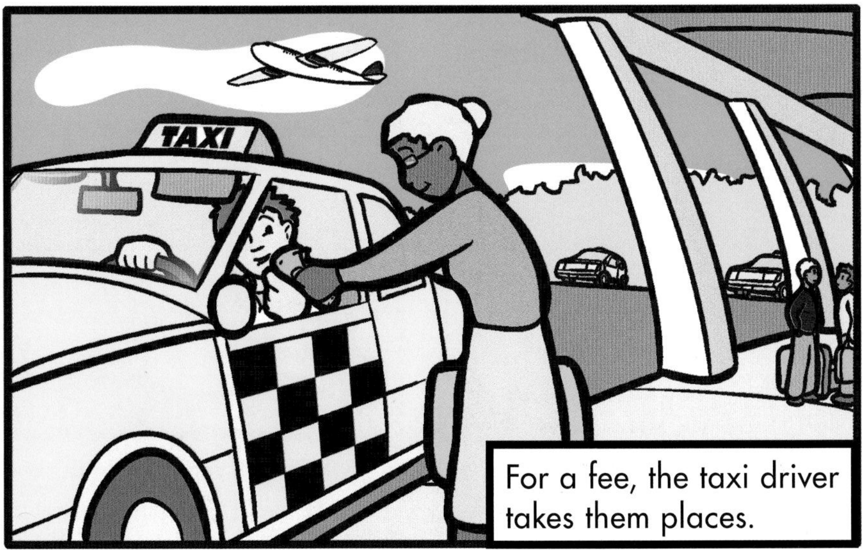
TAXI
For a fee, the taxi driver takes them places.

TRANSPORTATION FOR ONE

Crystal's legs are her transportation. By walking, she and her mom avoid traffic jams. They get exercise too.

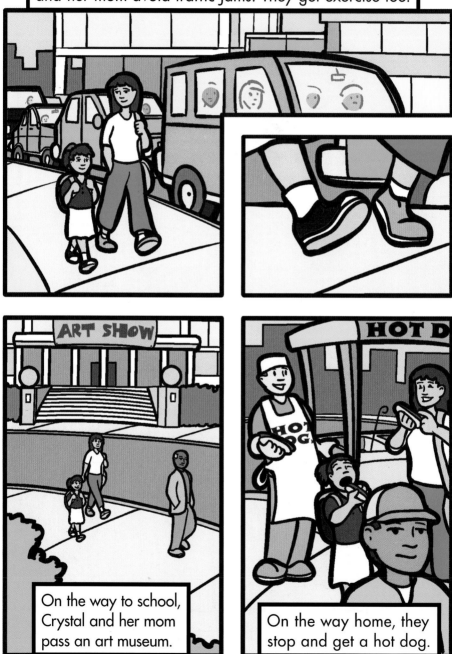

On the way to school, Crystal and her mom pass an art museum.

On the way home, they stop and get a hot dog.

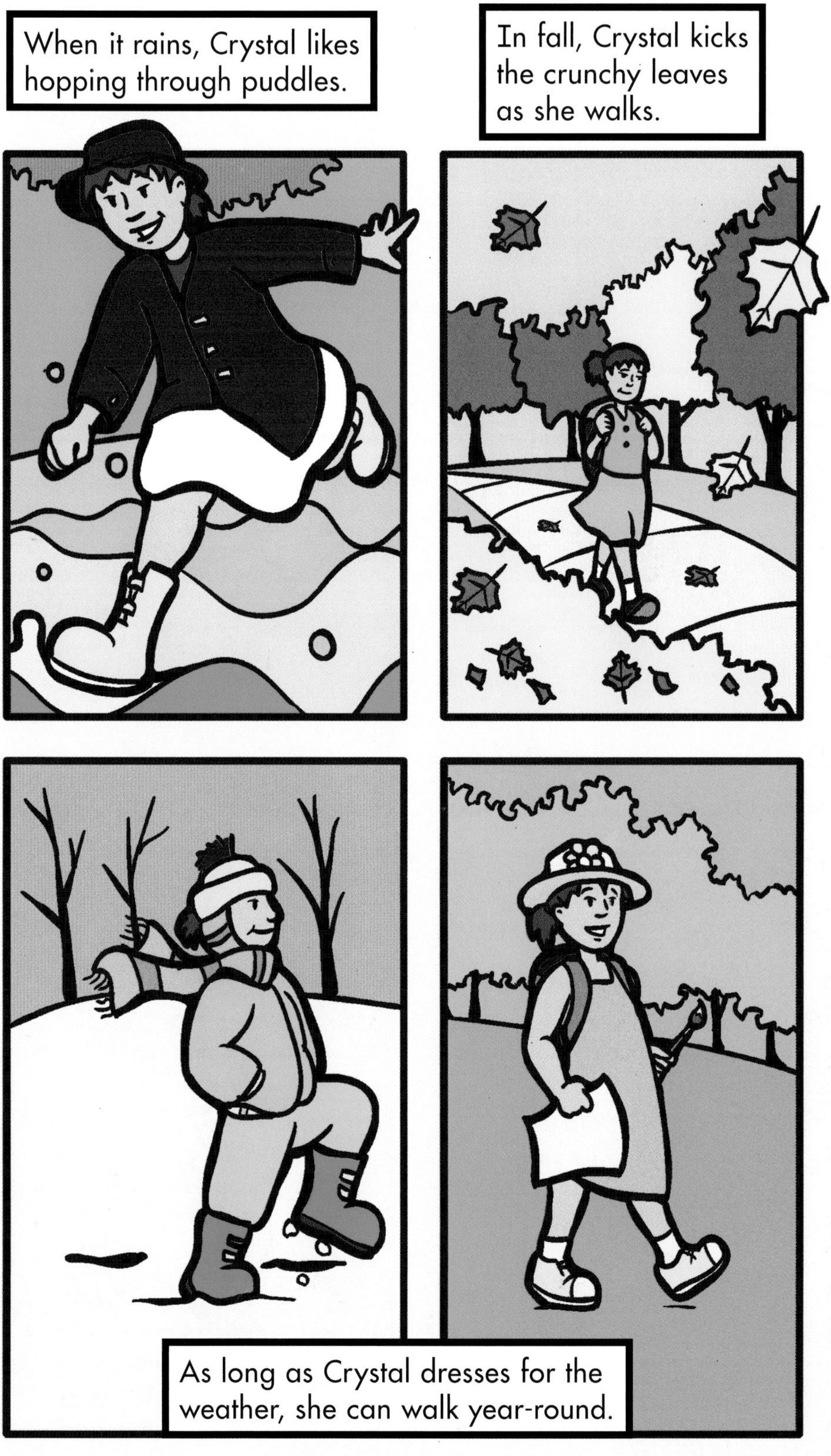
When it rains, Crystal likes hopping through puddles.
In fall, Crystal kicks the crunchy leaves as she walks.
As long as Crystal dresses for the weather, she can walk year-round.

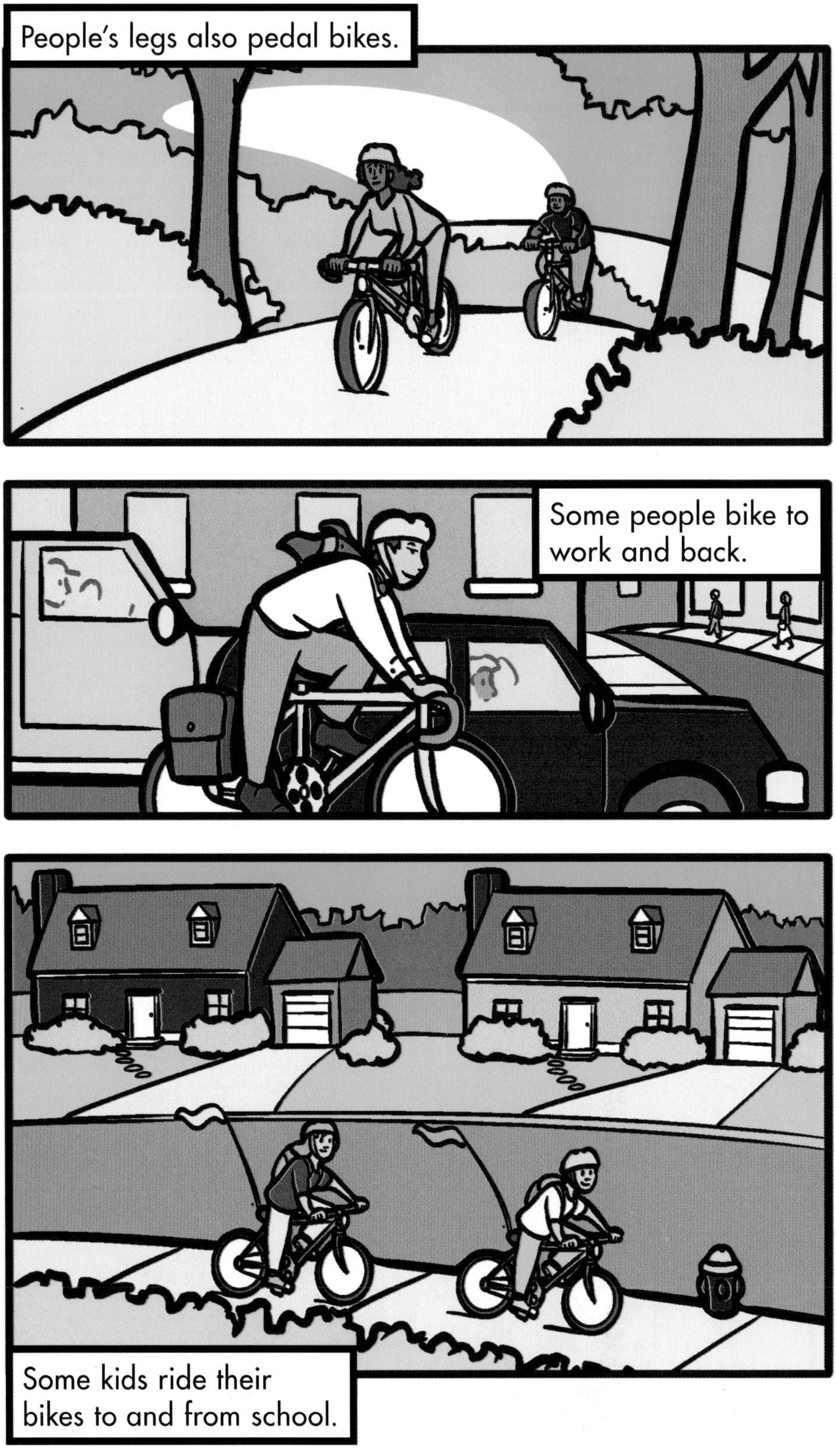
People's legs also pedal bikes.
Some people bike to work and back.
Some kids ride their bikes to and from school.

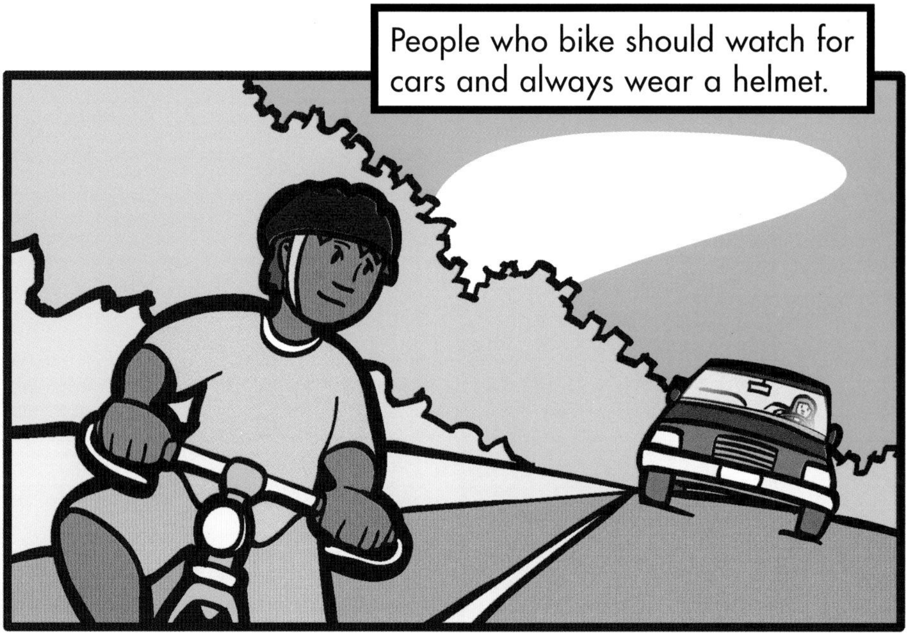
People who bike should watch for cars and always wear a helmet.

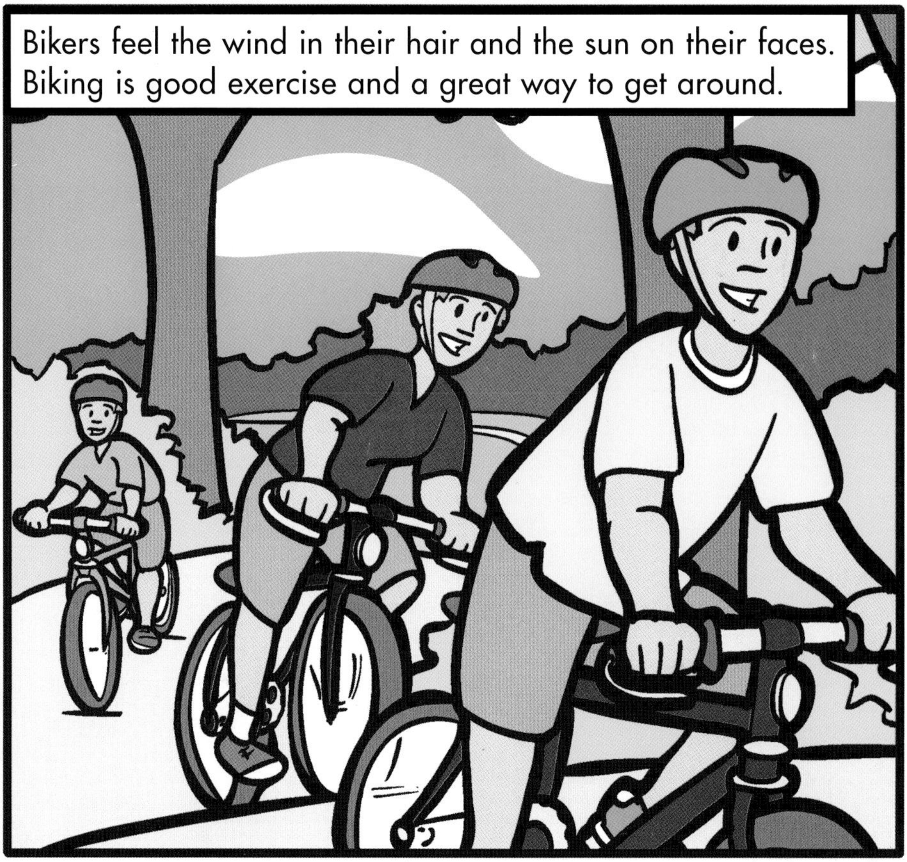
Bikers feel the wind in their hair and the sun on their faces. Biking is good exercise and a great way to get around.

Some people ride buses, trains, or ferries.

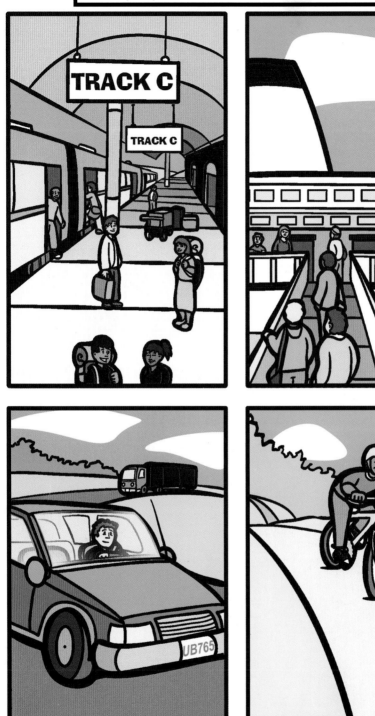

Others drive cars, walk, or bike.

Not all communities have all kinds of transportation.

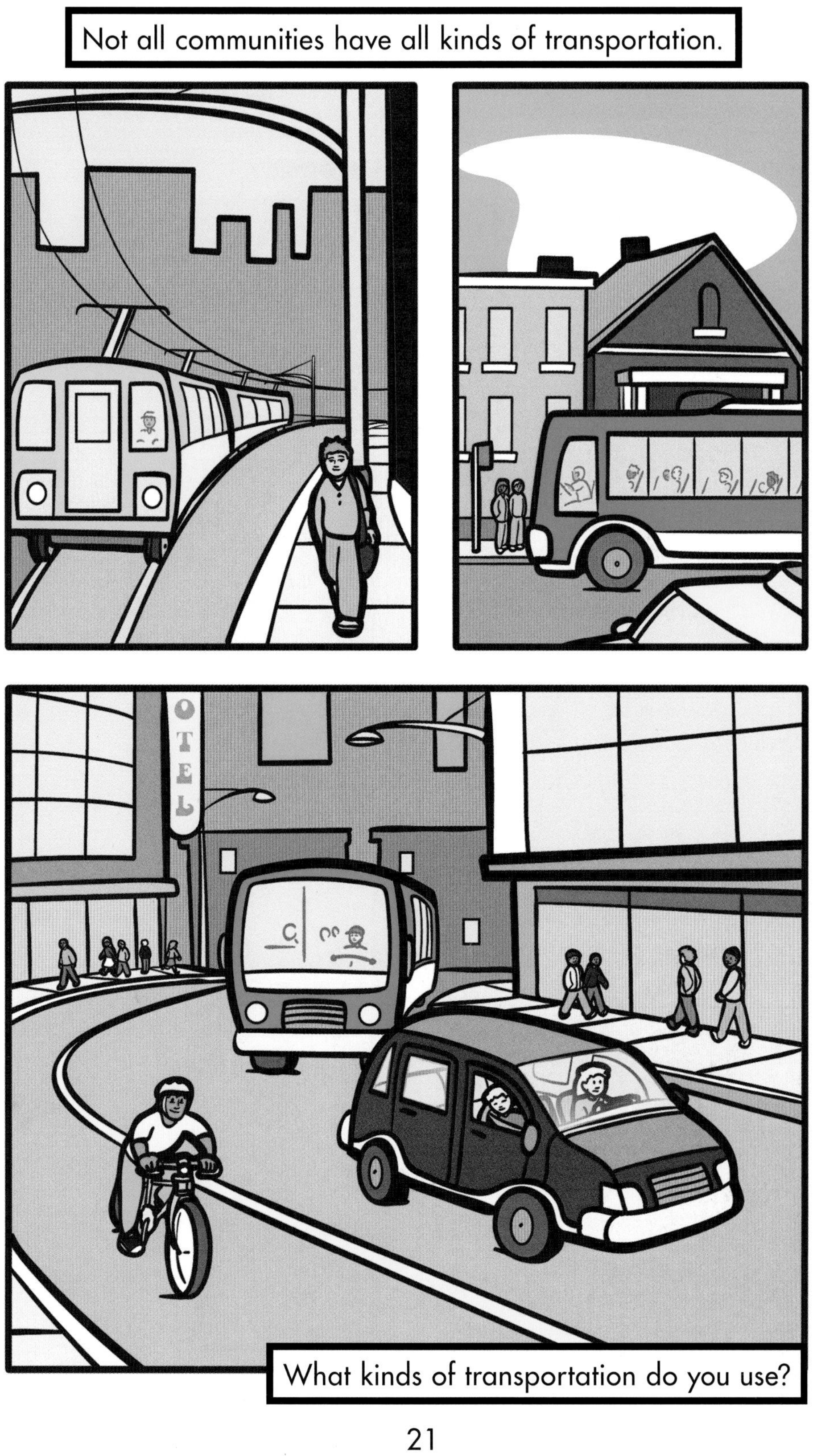

What kinds of transportation do you use?

GLOSSARY

carpool—to share a ride in a car with another person or people who are going to the same place

fare—the price charged to transport a person

fee—a payment made to someone

passenger—a person traveling on a vehicle

platform—a raised, flat surface

route—the road or course followed to get somewhere

READ MORE

Miller, Heather Lynn. *Subway Ride*. Watertown, Mass.: Charlesbridge, 2009.

Oxlade, Chris. *Bicycles*. Transportation Around the World. Chicago: Heinemann Library, 2008.

Rustad, Martha E. H. *Transportation in Many Cultures*. Life Around the World. Mankato, Minn.: Capstone Press, 2009.

INTERNET SITES

FactHound offers a safe, fun way to find Internet sites related to this book. All of the sites on FactHound have been researched by our staff.

Here's all you do:

Visit *www.facthound.com*

Type in this code: 9781429653701

Check out projects, games and lots more at
www.capstonekids.com

INDEX

MY COMMUNITY

TITLES IN THIS SET:

A DAY AT THE FIRE STATION

GOING TO THE DENTIST

TRANSPORTATION IN THE CITY

A VISIT TO THE LIBRARY

A VISIT TO THE POLICE STATION

A VISIT TO THE VET

WORKING ON THE FARM

FIRST GRAPHICS

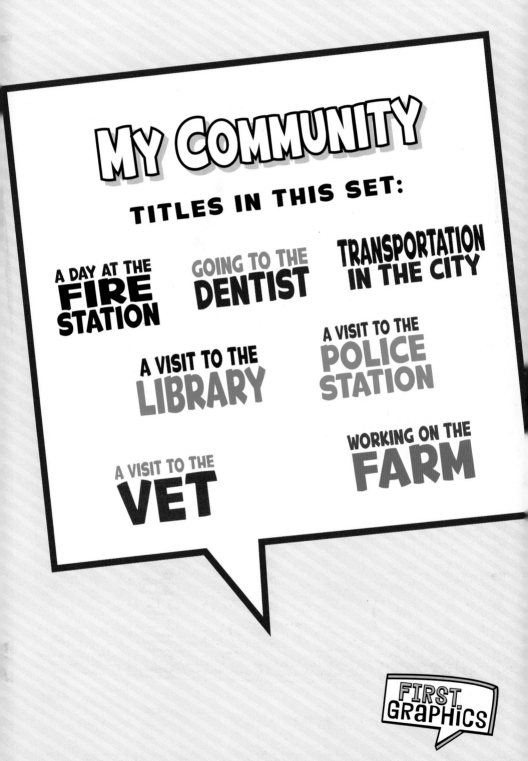